The Big Sand Dune

and The Beach Lady

on an African American Beach

March 11, 2014
Annette McMyers

Annette McCollough Myers

Layout by Jennifer Wehrmann

ISBN: 978-1-934666-50-0

Published and distributed by:
High-Pitched Hum Publishing
321 15th Street North
Jacksonville Beach, FL 32250

www.highpitchedhum.net

High-Pitched Hum
Publishing

Reading is the key to learning and understanding.

This book is designed to encourage reading among school age children and others to learn more about local, state and national history.

HISTORIC AMERICAN BEACH

American Beach was established in 1935 under the leadership of Abraham Lincoln Lewis, one of seven co-founders of the Afro-American Life Insurance Company, and one of Florida's first black millionaires. His vision was to create a beach resort as a benefit for company executives and as an incentive for employees to exceed in sales. Florida's beaches were racially segregated until the passage of the 1964 Civil Rights Act. Because of this, American Beach became regionally popular since it was one of the few beaches in the Southeast open to African Americans. Other sites in American Beach trace their history to the Civil War era. Amelia Island was home to several Sea Island cotton plantations, including the Harrison Plantation. In 1862 Union Forces captured Amelia Island and the freed slaves founded Franklin Town at the south end of this island. The Franklin Town cemetery, which had been given by the Harrison family to their slaves as a burial place for their families, still exists today on the west side of Highway A1A. In 1972, encroaching development forced Franklin Town residents to move north to American Beach. Their Methodist Church, built in 1949, was also moved here, where it now serves as the church's fellowship hall.

FLORIDA HERITAGE LANDMARK
SPONSORED BY THE AMERICAN BEACH PROPERTY
OWNERS' ASSOCIATION, INC.
F- 417 AND THE FLORIDA DEPARTMENT OF STATE 1999

1865 - 1947
Abraham Lincoln (A.L.) Lewis
Courtesy Florida State Archives

The Beginning of American Beach

American Beach is a famous beach. In past years, it was one of the few beaches for African Americans in the southeast United States when they could not go to other beaches.

Today, American Beach is the only African American seaside community in the state of Florida. In 1990, American Beach earned its first landmark in history when it became the northernmost site on the Florida Black Heritage Trail. The Beach was founded on January 31, 1935, under the leadership of a black man known as Abraham Lincoln (A.L.) Lewis. He also had helpers.

Afro-American Life Insurance Company
Courtesy Eartha White Collection, Thomas G. Carpenter Library, University of North Florida, Jacksonville, Florida

A.L. Lewis was known as the richest black man in Florida in those days. At that time and for many years, Mr. Lewis was president of the oldest African American insurance company (1901) in the state of Florida, called the Afro-American Life Insurance Company. The insurance company was located in the city of Jacksonville, Florida.

On January 28, 2002, American Beach was listed in the National Registry of Historic Places.

Photo by James Robinson

The Big Sand Dune

In northeast Florida on an island called Amelia, you will find the big sand dune.

Lewis Street Entrance Sign

The dune is found inside a small historical African American seaside community called American Beach.

Burney Road Entrance Sign
Photo by James Robinson

The sand dune on American Beach is the tallest dune found on Amelia Island and in the state of Florida. It is 60 feet tall. You can stand at the very top of the dune and see parts of the community, nearby communities, and the Atlantic Ocean.

Photo by James Robinson

Today, the big dune is not as tall as it used to be because it has been damaged by strong winds and hurricanes, but it is still huge.

Over the years, vegetation such as sea oats, other grasses and plant life have overtaken parts of the big dune. This is good because the plant life helps to hold the sand together.

Years ago, when parents and families visited American Beach for their children to play in the sand and surf, many parents would let the children play up and down the big sand dune. And, oh boy! Did they have fun! The children would be in their bathing suits and all covered with beautiful white sand from head to toe.

My mom and her grandchildren in 1963.

Photo by Maggie McCollough Carey

The Beach Lady

Courtesy The Florida Times-Union, Jacksonville, Florida

A Great-Granddaughter

Mr. Lewis, the founder of American Beach, had a great-granddaughter. She loved the sand dune more than anyone. Her birth name was Marvyne Elisabeth Betsch that later became MaVynee (pronounced Maa' Veen) Oshun Betsch. From time to time she would change the spelling of her first name by dropping or adding letters for various reasons.

Marvynee

MaVynee

MarVynee

Mavynne

Marvyne

Mavynee

The Beach Lady

"Getting the most from the least and living peacefully in harmony with nature is the most rewarding lifestyle."

MaVynee was a very interesting and unusual person. She was brilliant and mystical at the same time. She admired the life of a butterfly. Many of her posed pictures looked like a butterfly. She loved calling herself "Beach Lady." Neighbors knew her as MaVynee. Outsiders knew her as the "Beach Lady."

People would stare at her or come to the beach to see what she looked like or to take pictures with her. Some people were suspicious of her, because she was very, very friendly, very talkative and had a high-pitched voice.

Some people were afraid of her, because they thought she had supernatural powers and could turn you into different things or put you in a spell.

The Beach Lady
Courtesy Amelia Island Museum of History

In winter and summer, she dressed in cape-like ponchos, sweatpants, colorful headscarves, and beach thongs. She was tall and slender. She had foot-long fingernails that she wore in plastic bags. Her hair was so long, it was down to her feet. Her hair and scarves were covered with all kinds of political buttons and other colorful decorations.

MaVynee was known in many ways as a nature lady. The "Nature Lady" cherished the sand dune and the ocean. She believed in protecting the animals, the birds and bees and other wildlife. Some people say she inherited a small fortune of money from her great-grandfather and gave it away to save the birds and other creatures of the environment.

Recreational Vehicle Museum

The Beach Lady did not own a real house. She lived on other people's property, or on the beach. At one time, she owned and lived in a small RV that she turned into a museum. She wanted the beach community to be preserved for nature and wildlife and to protect the community from overdevelopment.

The Beach Lady was a vegetarian. She said she did not eat anything with two eyes. If you found her eating, she would always offer you some of her food or offer to prepare a vegetarian dish for you.

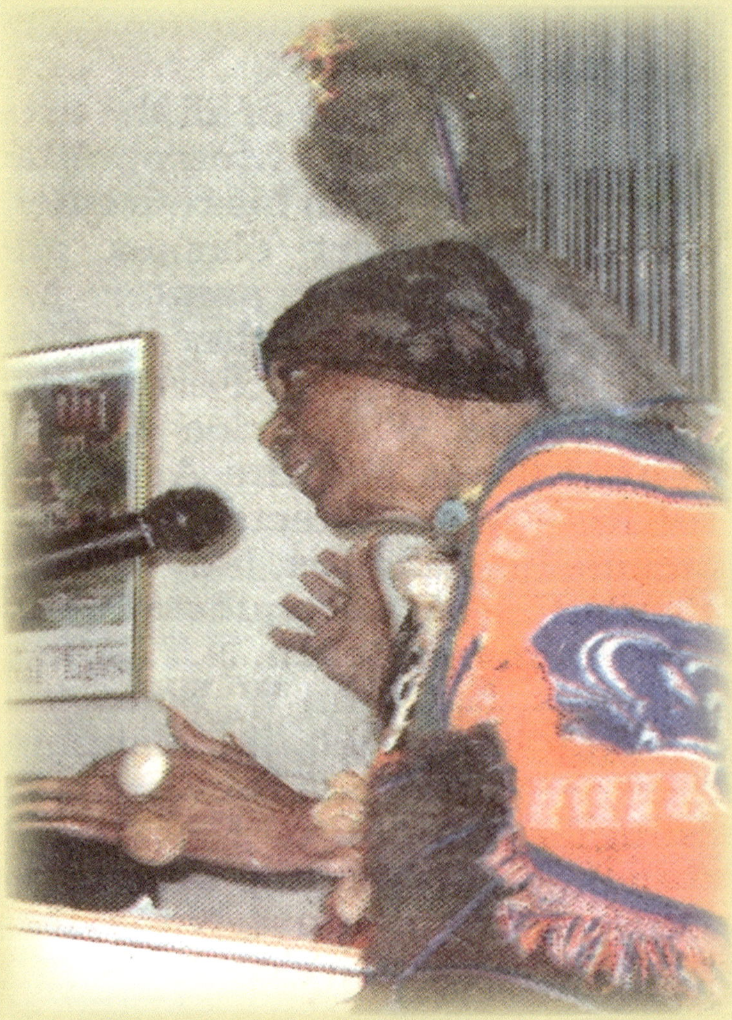

Courtesy Fernandina Beach News-Leader

Since MaVynee loved American Beach, she talked about American Beach everywhere she went. She named the big sand dune "NaNa." She said the name meant "grandmother" in African terms. The sand dune was sacred to her. She believed the sand had healing powers and could heal you.

MaVynee, the Butterfly, Beach Lady, Right Whale Number 1151,* Nature Lady, Opera Singer, died at American beach on Labor Day, September 5, 2005, at the close of the beach for the summer season. She was born in January 1935, the same year and month the African American beach was founded. Her ashes were spread on "NaNa," the big sand dune, and into the Atlantic Ocean on American Beach. Yellow flowers were also cast into the ocean as a farewell tribute.

** A whale named for the Beach Lady by biologists in the 1990s. The Right Whale is considered to be the most endangered of all whale species.*

MaVynee often told neighbors that, after she died, she wanted to come back to earth as a butterfly.

Many beautiful butterflies have been flying around American Beach. Wonder which one is MaVynee?

Interesting Facts

In 2004, the historic 8.5-acre sand dune, once owned by American Beach, was given National Park Service protection under legislation signed into law by former President George W. Bush. The oceanfront dune was donated by American Beach neighbors, Amelia Island Plantation, to the National Park Service in honor of the "Beach Lady."

"THE BEACH LADY HIGHWAY" was dedicated by the Florida Legislature on September 4, 2006, from Lewis Street to Burney Road south on Amelia Island's First Coast Highway.

On April 18, 2009, a State of Florida historical marker was dedicated and unveiled at the foot of "NaNa" for MaVynee the "Beach Lady."

The "Beach Lady" will be long remembered among the many people who knew her.

NOW THAT YOU HAVE READ THE STORY, HOW ABOUT A LITTLE FUN QUIZ?

1. In what state is American Beach located?
2. On what island is American Beach found?
3. On what beach will you find the big sand dune?
4. In what year was American Beach founded?
5. What makes American Beach famous?
6. Who founded American Beach?
7. Did the founder have a great-granddaughter?
8. What was the great-granddaughter's name?
9. Did she have other names?
10. What were some of her other names?

11. Why were some people afraid of her?

12. What kind of vehicle did she live in at one time?

13. Why was she called a vegetarian?

14. What did she name the big sand dune?

15. What did the name mean?

16. On what holiday did she die and in what year?

17. Where was she buried?

18. What did she want to come back to earth as?

19. Who wrote the story about *The Big Sand Dune*?

20. Where does the author live?

Answers: 1. Florida 2. Amelia Island 3. American Beach 4. 1935 5. It is historical. 6. Abraham Lincoln Lewis and others. 7. Yes 8. MaVynee Betsch or MaVynee. 9. Yes 10. The Beach Lady/Nature Lady. 11. People thought she could turn you into different things. 12. RV 13. She did not eat meat. 14. NaNa 15. Grandmother 16. Labor Day 2005 17. The sand dune and the Atlantic Ocean on American Beach. 18. A butterfly 19. Annette Myers 20. American Beach

Geographical Maps

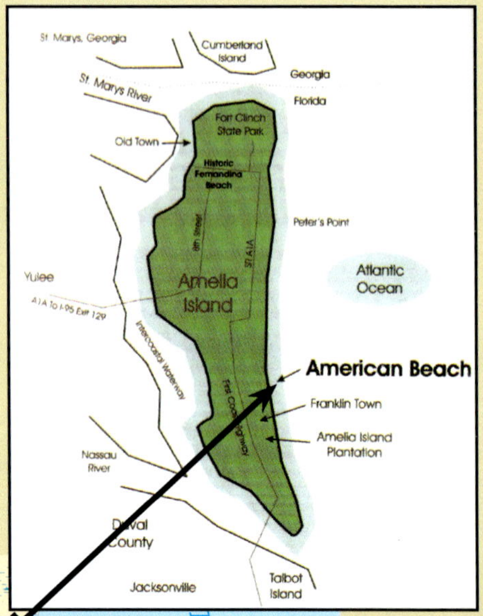

Inset Map Drawn by Jan Johannes